DANIEL BUINAC

Best Consumed in Contemporary Moonlight

Poetry of Falling Frames

Book 1

Globland Books

Published by Globland Books
Copyright © Daniel Buinac 2014

All rights reserved

The right of Daniel Buinac to be identified as the author of this work has been asserted by him in accordance with the Copyright, Designs and Patents Act 1988.

ISBN 978-0-9569634-4-4

Condition of Sale

This book is sold subject to the condition that it shall not by way of trade or otherwise be lent, resold, hired out or otherwise circulated without the publisher's prior consent in any form other than that in which it is published and without a similar condition including this condition being imposed on the subsequent purchaser.

Cover photo by Liis Roden

Contents

Scenery

Darkness in the Room 7
Perhaps we Wander… 8
Sometimes 9
Farewell 10
Bridge 11
July 12
And You? 13
Insight 14
Horrified by the Emptiness 15
Longing 16
Insanity 17
Silence - Before Departure 18
City Melody 19
March 20
Fatigue 21
Awakening 22
Dilemma 23
Dot on the Paper 24
It Will be Easier by Far 25

Story

morning coffee 27
when somebody whistles 28
I will confess perhaps 29
I ate my neighbour's piano today 30
on the outskirts of centuries 31
in this movie 32
should some space be left to mistrust 33
will be a long night 34
I saw fog with your eyes 35
nobody's calling for three days 36

I want to tell you 37
no need to apologise 38
just wish and you are there 39
it's not snowing outside 40
your shadow is suggesting a slow ride 41

Tribute to Fragments

before the attempt 43
hand palm 44
behind and under 45
the look follows 46
pain 47
the second night 48
without introduction 49
detail which sells the painting 50
not alone 51
they feed my restlessness 52
washing the horizon 53
in the current 54
sketch for restlessness 55
alone as never before 56
what we call time 57
exit 58
on longing 59
warm scenes melody 60
cautious 61
there was that too 62
at the gallery end 63
leave and don't question 64
I reduce you to space 65
and this night too 66
the end 67
I just craft some boats 68
dropped painting 69
let me be there too 70
and the answer 71

4

Best Consumed in Contemporary Moonlight

Scenery

Darkness in the Room

out of the music core
a faceless mass of screams.
imprisoned world's eyes
behind the window.
loneliness scent.
dust under the bed - eternity
fragments.
years lost.
sweat.
final scenes
of the stolen role.
spider's patience
until the curtains close.
peace
of already finished webs.

Perhaps we Wander...

Perhaps we wander in emptiness.
Abandoned,
perhaps we don't even move.
Perhaps we dream.
Voices.
Names.
Smells.
Stain each other with hands.
Step on each other with words.
Stumbling into each other in vacuum.
Perhaps happy.
With our eyes closed,
are we still here?

Sometimes

Sometimes I know.
I shape clouds with my hands,
north is my coat
and verses my raft.

Sometimes I remember;
licking forest dew,
asking eyes if they'd ever see
what my mouth just tasted.

Sometimes,
just before a rainy sunrise
while I lie alone,
I lend my voice to a hoarse rooster.

Sometimes, when weed
is fed with reality
a step of hope echoes
dully through the life,

but, sometimes, I turn off the light
and I feel; she is my...
And I dream.
Sometimes.

Farewell

Is that a part
that you chose to play?
Is that an excuse
you are avoiding to use?
You are quiet. I can't know.

Oblivion?
Is a candle enough
for forgiveness?
You burn in
my words' flames. Eyes
fixed on the floor.

Solution's shadow is lost
in your foggy silence.
Day at the finish.
Wind is good.
In your eyes
my open sails.

In this scenario,
who leaves first?

Bridge

Through a dirty bus window
I watch the dawn of the afternoon
dream.

Stranded by the vision
of an artist without a palette,
bound by the hand
of a devoted creator.

On the surface,
lifted from depths
by mighty current,
freed from blue darkness,
the world has eaten yesterday's day.

Forgotten and tired,
street lights
kill imagination
with their equal spacing.

July

Triangle of sand, sun
and move-on need.
Sweaty forehead,
tired eyes.
Thirst.
Today is desert.
Yesterday – swamp.
Wild at the beginning,
dried with impatient steps,
calmed in the family album.
Tomorrow perhaps steppe,
perhaps conifers.
Wind brings smell of salt.
Time wiped out the horizon.
Yet,
there is a sea out there.
(with an island for two)

And You?

And me?
I became cruel,
in my mind at last
tough. Mean.

And me?
Looking at your
photos and not noticing
years. Decades.

And me?
In vain.
Wandering the streets. Drunk.
Alone.

Not asking about you.
(And you?)

Insight

Soaked square full of laid down shop windows
Footmarks - sand grains
with enlarged faces
Eyes
Wind makes time visible
Unrealistically small space
Unrealistically free thoughts
Play

When we leave what do we take

Only people we met
once in our lifetime
live forever

Like the smiling faces
of the poster
on the coffee shop wall

Horrified by the Emptiness

glorious painting with a ruthless motif.
plush dream of a dying wind.
in the mist
movement to the centre.
deceived end.
opposite each other.
seemingly around.

Longing

Yet another dead light
(unfinished blink of an eye)
in this town.
Through long fingers of the night
leaks anxiety
grey as guts,
bitter as poverty,
dog without hair
at the fear door,
rust on a dream
that smells
like grandma's cookies,
like a dawn
and blues…

Insanity

You say:
only artless
is genuine
and you infiltrate my walls as damp
creep over my paintings
lick my colours
break frames with eyes
leave perfume in curtains
nails in my first canvasses
hair in my best paintbrushes

You say:
only splash is poetry

Silence - Before Departure

Genuinely liberated
and with staring eyes,
genuinely dry tonight
and next to the big river,
dry for a touch, comfort,
summer dusk and
genuine words,
I am thinking...

Genuinely thinking.

City Melody

Lustful morning on the worn out horizon.

Merely witness.
Merely dry wood.
Merely honour.

Broken bench in the park.

Merely roasted coffee smell.
Merely hunger.

Warmly dressed people. Where to?

All is merely
a dream.

March

In the awakening city
we looked at each other, tired.
The last sanctuary
from rising waters.
　Four letters...

City.
Burning paintings
curse their stillness.
　Void between them.
How long?

City.
　On my lips.
We disappear in a wave
of noise.
Salty.
　Forever
water.

Fatigue

darkness
full of boiling silence.
hotel room with
metropolitan-coloured stink.
final form of pain.
on my back.
she's lying next to me.
smoking.
december between us.
white.
rejective.
wiping her tears
with his cold fingers.
breaking the silence
with clumsy kisses.
carries her away.
lazy,
I refuse to move my eyes.

Awakening

Looking at the frames
of dusty years,
slow in appreciation
of rushing paintings,
we forgave others,
judged ourselves
looking for comfort
in the punishment.

Morning coffee smell,
milky mark
on heaven's face,
warmth in understanding
the necessary silence.
Gradated closeness
of frightened happiness.
Obscured
stripes of dissonance
in a mass of light.

With closed eyes.

In bed,
hugged by darkness,
time awareness
constraining the imagination.

Brutal over the
sinking ship.

Dilemma

Is it worth an effort
scratched night
blue verses
waiting
What will the flame tell me
(wires
branches
and a yellow beak
hungry)
Is one worth an answer
if one can't
anticipate it

Dot on the Paper

Dot on the paper is smiling.
Filthy capitulation conditions.
Surrender magic
And revenge absurdity.

She keeps looking at me.
Empty.
Made of patches.
Silent.

It's getting too tight
in the melting space.
She yawns.
Smells like Hyde Park.

I don't look, but I know.
She closes her eyes.
Too late for conversation.
Rain outside.

It Will be Easier by Far

it will be easier by far
to return the same way back,
crossed my mind while watching
the moon wandering among stars.

Story

morning coffee

morning coffee wipes
the sleepless night away
outside rain is melting the first mighty
snow after many years

surrender without fight
from my dream somebody is laughing at me
and the hand on the shoulder
I already forgot

I say you killed my hope
am I laughing too
or is it just an illusion
encouraging my restlessness

I say you won at the very start
is it interesting then to have
the triumphal line-crossing finish
isn't it easier to stop time

a coffee and another one
recycling impression
still raining
I say I'm glad for you

surely I should clarify some standpoints
perhaps give the snow a chance
although it should be pleased too
as I can't remember when it was so heavy

when somebody whistles

when somebody whistles under your window
and two crows are on the roof
next to the TV antenna
and the chimney

that doesn't smoke
while you write the letter
which you will never post
because tomorrow

the wind will wake up
and the sun will melt away the clouds
then you should know that all of it is
déjà vu

I will confess perhaps

I will confess perhaps
but first you must try much harder
nothing is free any more
nobody naive

but your TV is always on
how even to have a conversation
somewhere there only trees live
is it too late already

I ate my neighbour's piano today

I ate my neighbour's piano today
around six p.m. after he played
the false note for the third time
did any of the authorities notice that

after all these autumn rains
they are mostly concerned with floods
it's tough I know
but it's all in my favour

anyway the piano was old
perhaps it wasn't neighbour's mistake after all
there is the piano tuner of course
who should then be troubled by his conscience

I listen to the weather forecast
more rain on the way they say
it's not easy I know
but it's all in my favour

on the outskirts of centuries

on the outskirts of centuries
my dog and I
we used up all roads
that lead back

we look at what is coming
and what is already ending
or perhaps we even missed it who knows
what happened while the ads were on

in this movie

in this movie
you are supposed to be shy
with hands to cover your body
to be frightened, pure as you are

and not collect raindrops on the window
with your tongue
not to break the morning idyll
talking about them

how good they were
and how much you liked each of them
not to finish three
while I'm still on my first drink

not to laugh while I'm explaining
what you should be like
not to nurse my disappointment
with consolation

should some space be left to mistrust

should some space be left to mistrust
ahead of this conversation
I don't know
for far too long I haven't known you

won't be easy to say
that it is harder for you than for me
I'm afraid
it could sound cynical

perhaps everything will be fine
if I turn around three times
jumping on my left leg
or shall I believe that the crystal ball lies too

what an ugly occasion to talk
it's like we never
meant anything to each other
somehow I am ashamed

if you come at all
that's just crossed my mind
unbelievable
I am still naive

will be a long night

will be a long night
once it finally begins
with all unknown corners
in which yellow photos squat

ready to jump and with eager claws
leave marks
warm
visible only tomorrow

will be a long night
with all white sheets
which need to be written
by I don't know who

and which will be read to me
in the morning
as a verdict
before coffee and the face wash

I saw fog with your eyes

I saw fog with your eyes
while waiting for the bus
anyway that's not worth any attention
perhaps only when years go by

although the marks are still on the window
perhaps rain will wash them away
while we sink
in silence it's like I am hoping

nobody's calling for three days

nobody's calling for three days
I remember when she asked
if I remembered
and when I said no

perhaps they all actually have
something to do
it seems like a silly time
for the river walk

more so when the excuse is
search for the dog
that is missing three years now
how long since she's been gone

it's hard to remember
nobody to refresh my memories
they probably work and probably anything
any job will do in times like these

I want to tell you

I want to tell you
these ads drive me nuts
yesterday I didn't notice
today everything is

I don't want to exaggerate
cigarettes left on the bed
dirty glasses
sweaty chains

everything so rotten
it's like a century is already gone
and another one will
when the music stops

or at least the phone
not sure what makes me crazy more
bad rockers
or you

no need to apologise

no need to apologise
a hug will be enough
those who don't know us
will find it strange later insignificant

just look me in the eyes
if I could remember every second
is that forced laughter
or are we all somewhat sour

it could be we are not prepared
longing was hard
perhaps at the end short
later everything will be different

neither you nor I are guilty
or we are guilty only as much
as we blame each other
it's all the same now

we won't compare the pain
we are too well mannered
and if the first tear is mine
I'll hide it or share it

just wish and you are there

you wish and you are there
in a cold room with street lights
beer in your hand
next to you lies my dog

you think of old times and compare
you hear her in the shower
you are next
you wish you didn't exist

and it's snowing outside
everything is so predictable
hooray for the Grimm Brothers
you bottom up

my dog looks at you with compassion
she's singing you realise
there is no escape
you are in my skin

it's not snowing outside

it's not snowing outside
unfinished house across the road
taxi ignored a girl
in front of Odeon

I remember that night
I called them
and they said
just a moment please

laughter
it is a real pleasure to see
someone else at the window
majority is however unconcerned

your shadow is suggesting a slow ride

your shadow is suggesting a slow ride
and I am only halfway there
somewhere far away is my destination
I think I might be running late

surely it is damned sinuses
as soon as spring arrives
I melt
with the snow

and then I'm nervous
careless cat
brakes then accelerator
and you are not there any more

trying to relax
song on the radio
about a warm bed
and a beautiful woman

Tribute to Fragments

before the attempt

step that will get wet
and fat trains
that leave on time
and with time get bigger

hand palm

empty room dropped
like a glass on a way to marble
window
loneliness in various shapes
with tied wings
loses control over its senses

behind and under

in river waves bred
and tusks of memories - white
bridge to depth

the look follows

with ordinary words I paint
touch of hands
on their way
to an apple fallen off the table

pain

and so I see him occasionally
from that same terrace
as he grows on the horizon

the second night

wind in the linden tree's womb
everything is like the first time
everything like hearth
until the daybreak warmth of the answer
I stretch my memories

without introduction

under which stone
in search for a bait
will boy with black nails
find me
girl with fish mouth
and back turned to the moon

detail which sells the painting

from the mirror
silent line of words
frozen conflict
stillness
shrinkings
partings
caps

not alone

I have a night on needles
spring on sweaty palms
with last autumn rotten leaves
moonlight under the mask of dust
and closed door

they feed my restlessness

sleepy people with and without hands
concrete eyes
stumbling with their thoughts
tumbling food with tongues
and pulling words out of pockets

washing the horizon

while hunger feeds him
outcry from his eyes pours
down the street with rain
he is drunk
and they leaned him against a tree
so trams can pass by

in the current

deep down below the surface
surrounded by restless sea grass
and fish eyes
my memories like a lost anchor

sketch for restlessness

washed out city streets
in a night of invented reality
bareheaded lyrics
and darkened windows
silent until a scream of light

alone as never before

under the morning feet
thousands roofs of my house
jointly as one
building a tear in my father's eye
and nothing is ever as it was

what we call time

meat between teeth
left over from a nameless bite
to draw attention
price for the taste

exit

blind as maybe
sober as circle
which way to turn
to stay where I am

on longing

you are a fish with green guts
and horns stretching to russia
scared of walnut leaf
as it brings oblivion
(takes the smell away)

warm scenes melody

deep in my fingers
deep in my carelessly arranged shop window
where those passing by hide their eyes
from the world they tread with muddy feet

cautious

not every tap drips
three times a day I repeat
and it is still quiet
but I don't believe anyway

there was that too

with a silent choir
from year of emptiness
to year of vacuum
in an old man's hands
even older moon
pulled out of the fishnet

at the gallery end

I wait for sounds
while with frightened faces
they shake my shoulders

leave and don't question

because even when asked
an ant without half his body
will not let go of the straw in his jaws
perhaps he sees comfort in it
perhaps to ease the pain
perhaps to avoid the answer

I reduce you to space

here somewhere
here sometime
You see?
when I want to
where I want to

and this night too

linden tree ship under my window
with sails woven from the wind itself
and decks wet of impatience
that's me going home

the end

she was swallowed
by the platform three rush
she was swallowed
by a never-opened odour
of the train reeling towards tomorrow
ravenous tomorrow
running over the pieces of love still alive

I just craft some boats

I just craft some boats
and in them hide my rivers
from the sea

dropped painting

burnt time remains
warm farewell words scent
spirit silence
backgrounds
frames

let me be there too

let me be there too
let me tie the night
to thoughts of a dream
with your hair
so you can nurture the silence
on my palms
there is no past in the room walls
and your face can hardly be seen

and the answer

like a needle in the house foundation
remember my eyes
when I breathe in
the water

www.ingramcontent.com/pod-product-compliance
Lightning Source LLC
Chambersburg PA
CBHW020627300426
44112CB00010B/1229